The Algorithm Of A Culture

Márquez Price

Published in the United States by Márquez Price

Paperback

For more information,
Contact: marquez_prc@yahoo.com or www.mpricebook.com
First paperback edition February 2023

Dedication

To the people.

Table of Contents

Introduction

Like social media platforms have their own algorithms that show you more of what you're interested in, everything has an algorithm that shows you more of what you're thinking, feeling and talking about. When I say, "of a Culture," I mean black culture in that our celebration of the culture has become our destruction in the form of an algorithm. The algorithm is fed to us and then we perpetuate it without a keen awareness of how to differentiate between the effects of it. It has also served as entertainment along with monetization for others to copy and capitalize on. Black culture is one of America's greatest exports. This book is my own critical race theory that is applicable to all people regardless of their background because the primary objective of the book is to educate. This is my own dissertation. My doctorate in that I'm an expert in my lived experience as a black man- raw and unapologetic.

Banned weapon

Banned weapon,
double entendre.

Ammunition of the author—
lead shot from a sleeve,
lead shot from a barrel,
lead shot from a shaft,
varying by caliber,
semiautomatic,
a word at a time,
target practice,
on notebook paper,
from the pencil mightier than an AR-15,
America's rifle.

A country built off violence,
and the tilling of calloused black hands—
narrative from a constitution convoluted,
between killing,

and protection,
lawful purposes,
and self-defense—
no restrictions for the grim reaper's sickle,
when it wields at clubs,
wields at music festivals,
wields at schools,
churches,
mosques,
and supermarkets,
during the deadliest mass shootings in history—
during a traffic stop,
when a licensed to carry Philando Castile was killed on Facebook live,
not guilty—
and the largest gun organization remained mum,
but NAAGA spoke out,
to defend ourselves in this tempestuous political climate—
no ban for what my weapon writes,
with no ban for our weapon rights.

Melatonin

Tired of explaining—
to a color,
that being accustomed to privilege,
only feels like oppression,
when equality is demanded—
only as close to someone,
as far as you can work things out with them—
synthetic sympathy offers naught,
when black and white disparate experiences limit mutual understanding,
in the distance between the societal spectra.

Tired of worrying that erodes inner peace,
institutions that failed us,
and elected officials who used us.
Tired of seeing blue shoot red,
red shoot blue,
blue shoot blue,
red shoot red,

and black not acknowledging,
that the set is a terrorist organization,
when we voluntarily perpetuate our own genocide—
if every Monster Kody who twists their fingers,
and fly rags,
knew their warrior spirit,
wasn't intended to drop bodies in streets,
tribal instincts,
needed for a militia so the likes of Tamir Rice,
and Yummy Sandifer don't go extinct—
we are still spoils of their civil war,
where white casualties totaled more than any black-on-black killing.

In the school of life,
my class of millennials has tired—
our generation embarked upon the aftermath of 9/11,
systematic crisis,
and a pandemic at halftime—
while carrying the ball of burden with smothering student loans,
rocket trajectory housing costs,
and an omnipresent climate crisis.

The generation after is tired,
on Percocet, lean and oxy,

confusing entertainment with reality—
an escape from where love was never given,
because we were too busy taking selfies when social media swept us up—
it becomes hard to recognize love when encountered,
as intimacy has been swiped away by touchscreens.

Tired of us accepting the image of a savior,
the colonizer gave us,
desecration to indigeneity,
the consciousness of Christ wouldn't colonize a mind with an image of color,
my God looks like me if I was created in the image—
affirmations are prayers when I look in the mirror and speak 'em,
meditation is God-self talking to me when I close my eyes.

Tired of dark vs. light skinned niggas,
in behavioral separation,
or jest,
squabbling for superiority in a pigmentation contest—
we let the field,
and house dissension,
divide us down to the shade we date—
self-hate,

the darker you are,
the harsher your plight,
the lighter you are,
the closer to white—
even our melanin is tired,
we sleep on it like melatonin.

Colored only

Black love like Ossie Davis,
and Rudy Dee.

Black like the morning coffee my grandfather James
Barnes never integrated for decades—
he wasn't met with civility,
when they made him stand the entire train ride across
the country,
in his uniform,
coming home from fighting for your freedom in World
War II.

Black like the panther Chadwick portrayed,
before our brother transitioned to the ancestral plane.

Black like the ouch uttered from black mouths,
where the mother tongue cautions the taming of what
shall remain unaltered—
because good hair is natural.

Black like Medusa,
what seemed to be a scalp full of snakes,
Greeks had never seen,
as her dreadlocks were deemed—
not turned to stone,
in awe of her witnessed beauty,
they froze.

Black like the lips of my first love's kiss,
nothing more voluptuous since.

Black like the love of Nina Simone for black,
BLACK!

Black like civilizations absent every day in school curriculum,
because the invader wrote the history—
black like children who perform better in those schools than their counterparts,
when taught their own history—
results when self-confidence and love are cultivated.

Black like faces in America before Columbus.
Black like the whips,
with black seat leather we lean back against,
to push through black streets,

from a time when leather whips pushed forward against our backs.

Black like our barber shops,
underground railroads we frequent to free ourselves from societal alienation.

Black like W.E.B. Dubois,
and *The Souls of Black Folk*—
The Harlem Renaissance,
the writing of James Weldon Johnson,
Nella Larsen,
and Zora Neale Hurston.
The poetry of Countee Cullen,
and Langston Hughes—
paving the way for Ralph Ellison,
Richard Wright,
Lorraine Hansberry,
and Toni Morrison.

Black like the gun I vow not to brandish at another black body.

Black like our own cultural identity,
that doesn't need you to tell us who we are-
a culture sanitized after being stolen only to be presented as their own.

Black like economics that doesn't buy where it won't
be hired—
if we allow others to feed us,
we allow others to starve us.

Black like a people with financial trauma embarking
upon a financial revolution,
because we have no excuse now with the information.

Black like the knowledge we pass down,
generational wealth isn't just money.

Black like the cheeks guttered with tears,
sometimes our screams are cries,
muffled by the walls of an altruistic silence for others
to survive.

Black like the juice squeezed from words of the elders,
berries sweeter on the day understanding of them arrives.

Black organized like Marcus Garvey,
15 million Africans globally before the internet.

Black like the treaty of forgiveness we need to cease
our war within.

Black like families when the media omits two parent households that really exist.

Black land like ancient Kemet,
with fertile soil from Nile River floods—
dynasties harvested from the fruits of the original seed.

Black like alchemy,
the science of black people,
that started,
and taught other civilizations.

Black like Bastet,
before a black cat,
was bad luck,
the goddess of love kept evil spirits away.

Black like bellies of queens that carried us here.

Black like power palmed in fists raised to broadcast revolutionary propaganda.

Black like the onyx ashtrays old black men kept close to bed the squares they smoked.

Black like the ebony of trees we need to breathe,
black like the predisposition to high blood pressure,
Eucommia bark to relieve.

Black like the Bolt Usain was when he shot out the blocks.

Black like the blocks we try to shoot ourselves out of,
where bullets are administered on each other as antidepressants to depressed conditions.

Black like when they say we have a propensity for crime,
but overlook our reaction from dire straits—
black like politics with a prison abolition campaign.

Black like clouds that hover over us,
because we seldom have someone to pour out our problems to,
the stigma of seeking help becomes my mental straight jacket if I opt to remain strong.

Black like Miles Davis,
the Prince of Darkness.

Black like Bessie Smith,
Empress of the Blues.

Black like the consumers never considered to be citizens,
three-fifths compromise for their taxes.

Black like the culture America uses as one of its greatest exports.

Black like Jazz,
Blues,
Rock & roll,
Disco,
House
and Techno.

Black like code switching.

Black like jazz musicians started calling each other *man*,
because they were often called *boy* by others in the 1940's.

Black like a Berry,
Halle,
I'll forever have a love jones for her.

Black like you bet not walk in this kitchen without washin' ya hands—
Sunday dinners at the house on Linden,
before that movie Soul Food depicted—

black babies got put on the spot to lead in prayer to bless the food,
and black heads bowed,
or got popped by a black hand in Jesus' name.

Black like speak to black folk,
when you see black folk,
but all folk ain't kinfolk.

Black like two by the foot,
and two by the head,
in the same bed.

Black like hard candy when ya suga low,
hot combs burnin' on the stove.

Black like southern black-eyed peas with ham hocks.

Black like the homie Fresh who was never without a black and mild,
pulling smoke from black lips,
close to the grip of black fingertips,
at Cooley High,
where we gathered like black crows under the tree that we dubbed lil' Africa—
rollin' black dots on white dice,

and you owe me foe that bet,
black,
so run me my money,
Or I'mma beat ya black ass,
and most of us stayed out until the sky turned black,
because generations of black households were tumbling
faster than those dice thrown.

Black dreads,
Jack Johnson bald black heads,
black fades,
and black braids,
black kinky curls,
big black bouncy curls,
all natural fro like Angela Davis,
black French braids,
big black bun,
And black waves brushed into black hair with black
bristles—
from black beepers,
to blackberry a cellular,
to smartphones with the mineral Coltan mined from
black hands in Africa.

Black like rubber bands wrapped around rolls of cash
in shoe boxes,
slid under black shadows of the bed.

Black like gold fronts on crooked grills.

Black like hoppin' off the porch early in life,
to stand on the black of night street corners.

Black like slap boxing,
these black boys won't thump or tussle with you,
they'll shoot you now.

Black like durags—
I knew black boys could fly,
when I saw my brother DuJuan running to the bus stop,
with his flailing off the back of his head,
like a cape.

Black like barrettes,
Amber Good wore those on Tuesdays,
Afro puffs on Fridays—
I vehemently denied my crush,
when my mama pointed out how cute,
the lil' black girl was in my class.

Black like the graveyard shift outside,
that don't punch a clock,
hustlin' till day breaks.

Black like our churches,
where the choir moves your spirit even if you sit still on the surface.

Black like my grandmother Freddie playing dominoes—
you couldn't slam them bones on the table too loud,
because she ran the Estevan recreation center for the city,
and she was good enough to beat any player who didn't like her rules.

Black like dancing—
it's how we move to release the vibration of our battered joy.

Black like the charcoal under the grill of the barbeque,
not tryin' to hear your views while they smack on swine—
you can't push no knowledge on the one who didn't bring nothin',
but eats up everything.

Black like swisher sweets,
blunts,

and I'mma go upside ya head with the butt of this bottle,
at the park,
paper plates,
and foil for the classic picnic takeaway,
with influence of high cholesterol sized portions,
for diabetic palates.

Black like big poppa,
and big mama,
the youth went wayward when we stopped listening to them old folks,
and now generations after us won't hear us.

Black like take the garbage out or get woken up in the middle of the night,
cut them lights out,
and huddle up in the hallway when lightning strikes.

Hair rollers,
and house shoes,
you gon' catch a cold if you walk around barefoot.

Black like you gotta see me in person,
if you disrespected my name,
on sight,
no matter the location,

you gon' learn today—
we might get to speakin physically.

Black like always Jeffin',
get to steppin'
and stepin fetchit.

Black like rhythmic snaps,
Bernie mac,
proneness to heart attacks,
addicted to crack,
but black don't crack.

Black like black-on-black murders,
decline in America after police killings of blacks—
and there's no way we can't hear God's reasoning from within,
yet we're too caught up,
trying to convince America black lives matter,
when it's our birthright,
through displaced solidarity,
tricked again.

Black like I got a toothache so I can't worry bout your heartache.
Black like a people with no legislations or bill,

late on bills,
but I got all this designer shit on me when I pull up—
clothing my low self-esteem from when I grew up with hand-me-downs.

Black like a spiritual people,
if your vibe is off,
please believe,
we sensed it from the wind rustling the leaves in the trees.

Black like people in the hood who operate on a low frequency,
waking up daily with nothing to look forward to—
dilapidated buildings,
drugs we didn't source,
and guns we didn't manufacture—
fruits gardened in our environment to harvest our demise.

Black like smoke signals that rose from black bodies burning to warn others not to run,
we ran faster,
this plantation is not my home.

Black like the connotation in the dictionary that misleads,
they said vodou operated in ominous spells in order to quell our spirituality.

Black like being called judgmental
and self-righteous—
after learning to paradigm shift like Malcolm.

Black like for the people,
with red of the blood shed for liberation,
and green for the symbol of growth,
and fertility.

Black like I was the day I was born,
and black like I'll be until I die.

Black like the God of medicine,
Imhotep—
worshiped by the father of medicine,
Hippocrates.

Black like magic we use through language,
what a slave owner thought was us saying MASSA through broken English,

is Hebrew for oppressor,
you were never our MASTER.

Black like “bring her home,
if she can use your comb”—
because we weren’t welcome in theirs,
when the signs read **colored only**.

Black privilege

An advantage of immeasurable odds,
that gave the special right to overcome,
from scratch of nothing,
we nourished hunger pangs,
in a kitchen where failure is cooked up,
but never an option to be served.

Traded sweat equity for zero ownership,
as slaves who were the first stock on the market,
the hands of struggle in American ghettos have our people by the throat—
made us fit to survive through a simulation of capitalism,
in the streets next to buildings deemed projects—
shooed away by red lining,
pulled over by probable cause,
because,
your reasonable grounds identify my color as not your kind.

So used to our favor in being fucked with,
that we fuck with each other—
the crab is vilified,
until the crab learns who governs the barrel—
lift each other up,
instead of pulling each other down.

I talk loud through a vessel of ancestral spirit,
to speak a voice muffled in past lives of injustice.

I am unruly to deviate from a conformity you dress me
with to fashion your benefit.

I can live in a house that I built
against an exchange of a lie,
that says I am your guest—
because your nature is to take,
and mine is to forgive.

If my pain dared to wish for your comeuppance,
you'd regulate me with a label of *militant* to lessen the
fear of your wrongdoing,
but I escaped that captivity,
when I manipulated the misnomer of your stereotypes,
into the black privilege,

that grants me immunity to a struggle you still don't
understand,
because your privilege won't allow you to.

Gimme

Reaching for reparations,
from the bottom,
of the financial totem pole,
everybody got theirs,
never got ours,
to squander from lack consciousness,
so,
what—
gimme reparations in guns like Black Rambo TV,
that way,
nobody could rob me—
gimme reparations in dice game winnings,
we gamble daily though our survival anyway—
gimme reparations in index funds,
I'll let them sit,
and set it up for my kids to inherit—
reparations,
gimme—
multiple units in one big property,

for all of family members to live,
and rent out to others,
for extra profit—
gimme reparations in daily courses lead by Dr. Claude Anderson,
gimme reparations in Dame Dash's business acumen,
gimme reparations in every racial slur ever hurled at us,
I'll trademark 'em all,
and fine you every time you called me one—
gimme sparkly chains,
and luxury whips,
from nigga slang,
for the chains,
and whips,
the slave trader gave us—
gimme reparations in swisha sweets,
enough to blacken my lips,
and burn my fingertips—
gimme reparations in headboards for me,
and the Miss,
to keep breakin' 'em,
throughout the night,
because *if the bed keeps shaking,*
the house will remain stable,
African proverb—
gimme reparations in liquor,

enough to drink,
and wet the soil of the entire earth with,
to serve as libation for all the fallen soldiers—
gimme reparations in enough shoes to fill a stadium lot with,
and gimme reparations in closets—
chock-full of designer clothes,
we spend for the status symbols,
unable to enjoy real freedom,
materializing the symbols,
as an adornment of that elusive freedom,
even killing each other for the symbols,
from a feeling of worthlessness,
for things we consume as value—
gimme reparations in water to quench the thirst of Jackson, Mississippi.
Gimme reparations in peace of mind—
from anger,
grief,
exhaustion,
anxiety,
skepticism,
apathy,
constant triggers,
false hope,
shame,

and everything else,
we've learned to wade through,
in an adopted normalcy,
enslaved 275 years,
and then suffering 150 years of second-class citizenship,
of denied housing,
education,
loans,
and uttermost poverty—
12 million black men,
women,
and children,
killed in the Trans-Atlantic-Slave trade—
women gave birth on slave ships,
a breeding began,
on plantations,
to offset cargo shortage—
brothers,
sisters,
cousins,
and had to rape our mothers—
bags over our heads so we wouldn't know,
the origin of your *motherfucker*,
and we became descendants of slaves,
a people stolen from Africa,
with no nationality,

the very thing needed—
to receive reparations,
but—
gimme reparations,
because there was no United States of America,
before we built it.

Numb

A nigga getting killed in the hood every day is everyday shit,
dizzied,
and desensitized,
in our actions,
and mantras,
to where the entire world has become too desensitized,
to offer any compassion—
numb to our sickness,
because we lack concern for our own black death.

Lost so many,
we forgot how to cry,
numb.

Go another route,
and you get called a *sellout*,
die early,
and you get called a *real nigga*,
And a *real nigga* ain't nothing but a coward—

pointing a gun at another black man to kill 'em,
stock in mortuaries—
caskets we fill 'em,
nah,
I don't feel 'em—
but if that's the standard,
show me the REAL NIGGA—
who would jump in when they apply an Eric Gardner choke hold,
too busy extending a phone to record,
instead of a hand to help,
to send a video out for trauma bonding—
I CAN BREATHE,
for him to speak the truth to a real nigga.

Prophecy of Frederick Douglass,
"*It is easier to build strong children than to repair broken men*,"
and the broken men shoot the guns,
while a parent must explain to their 4-year-old,
that a generational curse sent a stray bullet through the window,
killing their baby sibling,
because we lack concern for our own black death.
Numb.

Tantrum

We protest,
I thought a zeitgeist deployed from quarantine,
behind his murder by the police in Minneapolis,
after the store clerk suspected a counterfeit twenty-
dollar bill was used,
but what we do,
is synonymous to a tantrum—
quick to burn out,
like the flickering flame of the lighter against the wind,
never ceaseless with meaning like deep-burning coals
throughout the night.

Feels like they're stiff-arming our foreheads,
while we swing wildly without connection until we tire,
catch our breath,
no results,
atrophy,
then repeat the same exercise,
in futility,

when the next black tragedy is propagated,
to manipulate our nervous system.

We protest,
without action,
but action,
is protest.

Protest with push up challenges—
to strengthen the temples,
our bodies,
and lessen our risk for heart disease—
because our men are 70% higher risk of heart failure
than white men,
and our women 50% compared to white women.

Protest by holding leaders,
and elected officials,
responsible,
while demanding that they change current policy—
attend city council meetings,
and organize stop the violence rallies—
because most of us listened to the platitudes,
and thought voting out forty-five was our salvation,
without understanding real change happens through
local legislation.

....

Protest by picking up trash in the community with the babies—
we're not excluded from environmental awareness,
and responsibility,
even if some of the conditions we live in are worse—
we still covet,
and purchase,
the phones,
that have the information,
to ensure our environmental justice also.

Protest by helping the elders without them having to ask—
Miss Mae,
Grandaddy Cornell,
and Sista Edna,
looked out for us in our villages,
before we left,
and forgot them.

If the best way to hide something from black people is to put it in a book,
protest by going to the library,
then start book clubs,
for book exchanges,

because knowledge is in books,
power comes from reading.

Protest arguing with each other over everything,
for nothing—
we accost each other over opinions,
willing to crash over trivial differences—
too busy comparing our GOATS,
over subjective matters,
that don't matter.

Protest by learning how to provide emotional security,
with each other,
in our relationships,
because many of us still equate love to psychological warfare—
our words abuse,
and our bodies collide,
bruise,
with makeup sex to bandage,
without any navigational guidance to an apology,
and we stubbornly island each other,
when forgiveness closes the gap of separation.
I saw a man heal,
when his mother hugged him for the first time—

he no longer could displace his neglect on the women
who tried to get close to him.

Protest by being better leaders,
I got friends who still hear the echo from the last time
their fathers slammed the door,
and never came back,
but they alchemized their pain,
into the prowess of Haile Selassie for the children they
raise now.

Protest by making your employer your investor,
until you can establish financial sovereignty as an
entrepreneur—
this generation has options now to break psychological
chains,
and the Willie Lynch prophecy—
How to make a nigger a slave,
they bred us—
I'll never call nobody "boss,"
on,
or,
off,
a clock.

Protest with your family by practicing group economics,
because charity starts at home.

Protest by learning your family health,
and mental health history—
it's no longer a generational curse,
if you know thyself,
to heal thyself.

Hydrate—
no protest is sustainable without water,
the blood of the planet.

Connect with a lover,
our people have adopted too much of the false notion
that going alone is the way,
lost,
like ebony zombies in the wilderness of life—
vulnerable to forever remain under siege.

Protest by protecting your family,
but remember it's better to live for 'em,
than to die for 'em.

Protest by finding a way to channel our fear,
or it will consume us.

Protest by disciplining ourselves to never give up,
because our ancestors had no choice.

Protest by knowing when to embrace solitude,
because our ancestors only had a modicum of peace.

Protest by listening to our bodies when we need rest,
because our ancestors never had that luxury.

Protest by sitting with people who cultivate peace within
themselves.

Protest by thinking more,
reacting less.

Protest by traveling,
by any means,
the world is bigger than the hood—
I saw a kid buy a case of one hundred bottles of water
from the store,
And from one hundred dollars he saved—
upsold each bottle for two dollars each,
during the summertime,
a few times,

and bought a plane ticket to fly across the country,
when not one person on his block,
had ever left the block.

Protest by correcting the system of unequal justice by
learning the law—
we break it,
and don't know it,
until we're studying for an appeal—
warehoused in that gated community up north.

Protest by learning to speak another language—
we've already mastered one,
not our own,
and remixed it with Ebonics.

Protest by forming hiking groups for fellowship—
we've lost our connection to nature.

Protest by planting a tree with our babies,
it shows us how legacy grows.

Protest by reestablishing our rural roots—
the city thinks the country has *bamas*,
and bumpkins,

but those people would be our only way to survive off
the land if our lights shut off.

Protest by abstaining—
weed,
liquor,
thinking prison is a rite of passage,
or whatever you define as a vice,
for 30 days,
to claim a moment of clarity.

Protest by never forgetting Kalief Browder—
I still can't reconcile the rage I felt,
and the comeuppance I wished for his captors,
after seeing his harrowing story.

Protest by training your body daily—
calisthenics,
and cardio,
to combat diseases predisposed to in your bloodline—
martial arts to combat vulnerability,
when no weapon is available,
for self-defense.

Protest deficient nutrition—
a piece of fruit,
and a handful of greens,
to start—
I saw my niece become a vegetarian,
with access to a father's cooking—
his love language,
that rivals your favorite soul food spot—
and he mainly eats salads now,
two years later—
on a subconscious level,
our children give us lessons,
we return love by changing for the better.

Protest by discovering health is also what you're thinking,
and saying—
so,
speak to yourself with a sense of value—
turn your words into wisdom,
and heal those who traumatized you,
by not becoming them.

Protest killing one another—
our people,
that are killing our people,
are enemies too—

deem it equal to suicide when you slay your own kind,
for we're the only people killing,
and rapping,
about it—
I'm still a hip-hop baby,
with a love matching what it was in my adolescence
for the culture,
but with a developed brain as a man,
to understand,
something is off about our genocidal anthem—
a death culture for the vultures to descend upon,
because lyrics served as commentary during my adolescence,
and lyrics reflect a lifestyle for adolescents now—
Biggie,
and Tupac,
was a catastrophe then,
rappers are murdered weekly now.

Protest the square versus street life dichotomy-
not being built for that life,
don't always make somebody soft,
and some of us got caught up,
trying to prove they could go across those tracks,
to compensate for the guilt of not having to live that life,
when inside,

many in that life,
don't want to live that life,
and would trade—
that's why they despise their prey.
Imagine one day,
when snitching in the hood,
was as deplorable as—
raping,
robbing,
assaulting,
disrespecting,
molesting,
and murdering,
our own-
even when you're doing something wrong,
there comes a time,
when your moral compass,
says you should stop.

Protest by building,
and keeping good credit,
how you manage money is how you feel about yourself,
our financial institutions like *Earn Your Leisure* have the tools for us to use.

Protest by finding your purpose,
it's a freedom never doomed to be taken away.

Protest by learning weapons training,
that teaches,
tactical approaches for when potential danger arises,
and loving our people,
is the remedy,
that will antidote the homicidal madness,
when we learn that communication is a more effective alternative,
because the disciplined know,
that you never show,
unless you intend to shoot,
weighed by the consequences of pulling that trigger—
and sometimes,
I feel like bearing more arms than black soldiers,
because Martin Luther King was our most powerful example of peaceful protest,
but they shot him too—
confused,
I don't know what to do.

My people remain quiet when we kill each other—
we wonder why they can't hear our cries,
otherwise,
because a tantrum,
is not action.

Real estate

Willing to die for a street sign,
all we have is psychological equity on the block—
dumb out,
run out,
in broad day,
another stain on the sidewalk—
fraught sounds from sirens,
the fuel of weariness returns the ambulance to a familiar scene,
a mother's screams,
brought the property value down,
then sold granny's house for nothing—
an asset she left you,
it was paid off,
we could have fixed it up for generations to live in,
familial haven,
or property to steward,
together,
and break bread,

off rental income—
the gateway to generational wealth,
from the echoes of once vibrant communities,
to the absence of—
schools,
supermarkets,
hospitals,
banks,
silence of the four essential institutions,
needed to speak *community* to our lacking dwellings,
run down,
for the devouring of gentrification,
on the corner hustlin',
gangsta pandering to the attention span of our people,
the information is available,
our lack of financial literacy has been our liability,
economics is the vehicle,
education is the key—
steady screaming where we from,
never seen anyone—
stand ten toes down,
to the asphalt reppin',
then turn angel,
and fly to heaven,
from the streets,
with a brick,

piece of plywood,
or slab of concrete,
when the dirt beds our flesh prematurity over drama,
but kin down south still maintain the seed,
and soils dirt to nourish that same flesh,
through a long life,
lost our way,
in time for navigational systems,
to guide our way back,
to no ownership,
perpetuated,
satisfied—
when we get the same street named after us,
that we died by,
our real estate.

Cotton

Picked it,
black battered bodies,
pain grasped achy backs,
that never bowed,
to merciless thorns,
with bad intentions,
and bloody fingers—
they handpicked the seeds,
out of the plant fiber,
burgundy stained,
cotton—
then made it into the fabric,
of the clothes,
we greed to possess today,
to aid our need,
from lack,
stalked by past shame,
of run over shoes,
and holey socks,

worn—
and worn out,
three days,
then flip them shits for four more,
to finish the week—
fists balled up,
to counter,
the combinations,
of those kids who throw jokes,
when the target walks to school,
consumerism—
driven by dissatisfaction,
we got plenty cotton,
covering those black battered bodies now,
back from the aches that enslaved us not long ago,
that drip—
spend more of our disposable income,
than anybody else,
with more buying power than ever—
1 trillion,
gross national—
2 percent,
we reinvest into our communities—
consumers vs. businesses,
a dollar circulates one time,
in our communities,

six in theirs,
and nine over there—
ashamed to support black business,
even though we're starting to create more black businesses,
overlooking black-owned retailers,
paid at 5pm,
and broke by midnight,
with enough cotton picked out of the closet,
to adorn the ugly hidden truth,
that we are unfortunately,
unaware,
that we are—
the commodity,
to this country's economy—
the crop,
the cotton,
the engine,
like the cotton gin—
that prolongs our own institution of financial slavery,
the longer we don't harvest our own literacy.

They say the sun is pro black

They say the sun is pro black,
its heat lies down on our skin tones like a cape—
born with more melanin,
the darker the pigment—
attribute of a superhuman,
to protect us from overexposure.

We seem to shun the sun,
and the warmth of our life generator,
we say it's too hot outside—
so,
slide—
that nozzle all the way to the right,
or punch that button,
not getting' in no car,
wit no AC,
but my grandfather AD Price never owned no car—

he walked everywhere,
with his feet as his rear tires,
his shoulders churning in front rotation,
as the wheels to guide his direction—
poppa said,
roll them windows down,
and take your vitamin d—
the adages,
of them ol' black folks,
reaching back from sweltering days,
sittin' on the porch to save us—
because we're no longer outside,
long enough to absorb the recommended amount,
produced by the sun.

20 minutes,
per day,
of sunshine—
triggers your body to release over 200 antimicrobials,
that fight fungi,
parasites,
and viruses.

They say the sun is pro black.

Its shine produces the happy hormone,
serotonin,
but the inner cities are still gloomy—
abandoned toxic waste sites,
loom around the corner of communities,
and toxic factory emissions,
with smokestack plume effects from coalfired power plants—
watch the babies so they don't eat fallen chips,
from lead—
poison in older houses.

They say the sun is pro black.

Conditions of sleepless nights,
heightened stress,
and weak immune systems—
the sunshine aligns benefits of all three.

Everybody loves the sunshine,
Roy Ayers on repeat,
but not all of us get to enjoy it.

They say the sun is pro black,
a people only pro black when we are in the sun.

Bully

I was a kid who liked to read,
and ride my bicycle,
cake mixing bowl full of Apple Jacks—
Saturday morning cartoons,
and niggas around my way wouldn't let me be myself—
speak a sound sentence,
they'd slap me upside the head,
and call me white boy—
I didn't even have any white friends,
never dated a white girl—
my bullies grew up in the same neighborhood,
same schools,
and teachers—
slapped the books outta my hands,
and whooped my ass on the daily—
turned me into something else,
armored myself like a weapon,
violence became my ammunition.

Fell into the neighborhood bullshit,
for the camaraderie of the hood,
neighbors no more—
I don't wanna do none of this shit,
but I wanna be accepted.

Selling dope,
dumbing down my vocabulary so they would embrace
me—
knew I was a square,
the wolves could smell it on me—
part of the pack,
instead of the hunted—
I became the biggest bad wolf,
the bully—
even the bullies feared me now.

I wanted smoke with this older head for rank,
the wrong one to play with—
got home,
twenty niggas in the living room,
he was sitting next to my mama on the couch,
with a handgun to her head,
magnum research desert eagle—
get your son right,
or I'mma bury him—

I almost threw my life away,
being something that I'm not,
a bully.

Religion

Rise,
to ritual,
on the daily.

Church service held device,
praying thumbs,
thumping that screen,
like heels against pews,
like Mahalia was singing in the choir.
Following who we worship,
tithes when we subscribe,
it's like a religion—
influencers preaching their gospel,
these selfies be the sermons.

"Likes" he gives on every post for her attention,
heaven if he gets her reaction,
but she feels like she's in purgatory waiting for a reply
from someone else—

perdition if the analytics show limited reach on them reels,
low self-esteem shrouded by filters,
and BBL's for everyone—
thirst advertising,
to slide in them DM's,
predatory personalities looming to stalk their wayward desires.

Unfollow,
and block those we don't know,
when they harass us.

Unfollow,
and block those we do know,
when fear kills potential conversation to remedy our differences—
power executed from a distance,
because the intimacy,
through proximity,
of human interaction seems to vanish more by the day.

Watch time got us like zombies,
scary statistics on teenagers tied to mental health decline,
adults no different—
too busy trying to keep with the Joneses,

to raise children—
this thing is engineered to be addictive,
each reaction,
and comment,
presents a small hit of dopamine to our brain,
let a glitch cut this shit off—
and it would pop off the apocalypse,
because we've become fanatics who can't live without it.

It's where the thugs now play,
the streets lost its way—
let some nigga trick you out your position,
said what you gon' do,
indictment online for everyone to see.

Lying on status,
tricked into mimicking what the algorithm designs,
grandstanding on live,
one upload from going viral,
mentioned by a celebrity in the notifications,
not here to socialize—
there's no love here,
disciple to that blue check,
this page is an ATM machine,
hashtag currency in exchange for that newsfeed—
tag,

and troll,
a path to the bag,
because everything costs,
and we gotta survive,
another way to monetize—
pimp the system,
welcome to my pulpit—
you are now my congregation,
pick your platform,
because social media has become our God.

Push

Push past shrinking yourself,
You are impactful—
the paintings,
monuments,
dynasties,
the essence,
and original recipe that the copycat studied—
we have left evidence of ourselves all over the planet.

Push past the barriers of limiting thoughts,
You are the architect—
we've been beaten down long enough through psychological warfare.

Push past the stigma,
You are healing—
we suffer from mental illness,
from our trauma,

this is a clarion call—
to more aspiring black therapists,
to administer our therapy.

Push past the obstacles,
You are a survivor—
we have leveled through every quest in the game of civilization,
through each opposition—
triumph through depletion,
our genes won't allow our disappearance.

Push past poor mentality,
You are rich—
and come from a continent of copious resources,
with 40 percent of the world's gold—
its why your love of jewelry is innate,
the drip,
and shine is in your DNA—
90 percent of its chromium,
and platinum,
largest reserves of cobalt,
diamonds,
and uranium,
65 percent of the world's arable land,

10 percent of the planet's internal renewable fresh water source—
you thought Wakanda was only a movie,
because our memory of our glorious home is scattered,
by our struggle here,
but the mother land has always been the world's reservoir to take from.

Push past your fear,
You are mighty—
like Gaspar Yanga.

Push past the uncertainty,
You are divinely guided—
your inner voice,
that connects to the divine when you listen—
Ye are Gods and children of the most high.

Push past struggle,
You are ingenious—
like our grannies who made gravy out of flour,
stirred to thicken from hardships,
and recipe what nots,
nobody's food was better because the main ingredient was love,
and that's how it fed everyone.

Ingenious—
like that kid who went to the military after high school,
cut hair for everyone on the base,
stacked his chips,
and learned stocks,
before leaving the service as a stock trade millionaire guru,
in his early twenties,
teaching millions by the name of Aristotle.

Push past scarcity,
You are abundant—
like that OG we called BRB,
"Be right back,"
used to pull up to the barbershop,
and push whatever you wanted,
or needed—
I learned how to cop something,
flip,
and upsell it,
watching him,
any request—
"I'll be right back,"
that trunk would pop,
and everything came out it,
as if it was a food truck,

or department store—
chicken wings,
car detail kit,
50-inch TV's,
Computers,
and merchandise—
started his enterprise from street pharmaceuticals,
left graveyard shifts on the block,
where he clocked in at the streetlamp,
to brick-and-mortar legitimacy in a plaza with a major
printing shop,
and a successful soul food restaurant down the street,
"You better have 7 streams of income,
because a job is JUST OVER BROKE,"
he put me onto George C. Fraser,
and his masterpiece "Race for Success,"
I soaked up the game.

Push past the need to follow others,
you are leaders,
the blueprint—
study the brilliance of our brother 19Keys.

I'm not writing to my people,
I'm speaking affirmations for my people.
Push.

I remember you

We elevated together,
when we meditated together.

The ancestors guided us,
safely when we listened.

Sirius was our night light,
sunrise—
waking up,
to the motion of our bodies that became morning
modus operandi,
in the Sahara Desert,
we moved when the season changed,
to start a family,
the offspring we raised,
that succeeded us—
their swimming pool was the Nile.

We disagreed fiercely,
but you helped challenge the granite,
that became the man I am.

I held your hand on long walks,
across the Serengeti,
before we were captured,
divine beings they tried to shackle,
living through this experience called life,
in a place where privilege renders us foreign,
spoke our own dialect in other lifetimes—
Swahili,
Zulu,
Yoruba.

The look in your eyes,
as you became evanescent on the horizon,
embroidered a fury on my heart,
when they separated us,
you were my Queen,
way before they tried to Slim me.

I found you again in the city,
Double Dutch between cars in the street,
you glanced over at me,
and winked—

my family survived the gutter,
yours was left wedged in the trenches of an epidemic—
I wasn't free,
while you were still oppressed—
we still managed to find each other,
at the park,
between being hunted,
by others,
and our own on this targeted map—
the stress became our lust,
for one another,
to get out,
and became two teenage parents,
who had to raise a child,
destined to begin,
at a reset of a game designed,
to move the sun,
moon,
and star,
paces backwards.

They don't understand us here,
their fear,
has helped deteriorate our unity,

but it can't be conquered by their system,
curated to knock us down,
and keep us down.

Jilly from Philly sang to me.

My love will always find you,
black as coffee beans,
when I look into your eyes,
today,
may we build upon each other's peace,
Black woman,
I know you've always been there—
you told me you were the one I was born to seek,
I remember you.

Blacker than you

You're not as black as you think you are—
the confession of an enemy,
revealed—
from the mouth of a trojan horse,
came from the heart,
his truth—
no longer shrouded,
in faux friendship,
flawed perception of a colonizer,
of what black is supposed to be,
mutated his insecurity,
from a primordial objective,
in that he couldn't look down on a black man,
who was the living compound interest,
of the struggle,
his ancestors surmounted,
his plotting—
was the harmful side effect,
and subterfuge,

of integration—
he thought I didn't know,
his questions,
weren't of curiosity,
but of reconnaissance
his jokes weren't of banter,
but of true feelings,
his boosting,
of living on the same street,
as killers,
growing up,
and closeness to a *real one,*
not from the city—
you told me what he said about me,
and I know you told him what I said about him,
tricked me—
into trying to convince you,
I wasn't his idea of me,
because we take our trauma,
and weaponize it for other blacks,
we feel aren't as *real,*
if they didn't endure the same harsh trauma,
from diametric upbringings,
was never your place to instigate,
your anger,
that ignited,

when I told you,
reciting Tupac lyrics,
bar for bar,
only allows you to dissect,
but not feel,
from the body we are as a people,
that our coast-to-coast prophet spoke for—
you couldn't see the slave auctions,
when I scoffed,
at your recreation,
of constantly—
wanting to compare,
black athlete vs black athlete,
black entertainer vs black entertainer,
you threw stones at my hero Ali,
by saying his principles paled,
to his cruelty to Smokin' Joe,
we loved both champions nonetheless—
I told you,
I outgrew listening to raps,
that depict black on black slaughter,
a boundary you overstepped,
the following day by marveling at a song,
of a young black man priding himself,
in *exterminating enemies like rodents,*
in a seemingly eternal battle,

where the exterminator has manipulated us,
to first see ourselves as rodents,
to exterminate each other,
for them—
from your seat of the coliseum,
that type of gladiatorial self-hatred,
doesn't shock your chakras,
but in your mind,
you are,
blacker than me,
I agree—
like that form of theatrical makeup,
used by non-Black people,
for Blackface,
to portray a caricature of a black person,
minstrel shows—
1800s,
your burnt cork,
and shoe polish,
to mimic us on plantations,
blacker than me—
I agree,
because when others come to our communities,
to set up businesses,
we welcome them,
but we are met with resistance,

when we try to do the same in theirs,
blacker than me—
I agree,
we traveled here,
before the discovery of Columbus—
Africans made voyages,
from west Africa,
through the Maritime Trade,
blacker than me—
I agree,
the ruse you gifted us,
to hate who we are,
and love who we are not,
to think if we act white enough,
we will be accepted by you,
blacker than me—
I agree,
Mama warned me of your kind long ago.

Aboriginal

The root of all civilization,
in the recesses of our memory,
self-esteem linked,
to the understanding of a history,
names like Kush—
the conquering generals of Europe named it Africa,
the alphabet,
mathematics,
and writing—
were the foundation,
for others to swipe,
and replicate once they arrived—
we were thriving,
the gold capital,
the wealthiest man on the planet—
A king in Mali,
named Mansa Musa sat upon his throne of riches,
stimulated economies,
with his generosity,

when he traveled—
there were powerful dynasties,
aplenty,
so many that we had thousands of rulership,
makes it hard to pinpoint,
they minimized it with tags—
of *mystery*,
and *myth*—
my grocery store was the land,
our own priests,
and medicine,
one race—
human,
the school is life,
Africa was the educator—
our bloodline stretches all over the world,
Hannibal Barca,
and his military genius,
The Moors salvaged your dark age,
brought hot,
and cold water,
lighting regions with lamps,
and building with architecture,
to create cosmopolitan cities—
Moor means *black*,
like the great boxer Tom Molineaux—

the slave who fought his way to freedom with bare knuckles,
called him *the moor,*
Benjamin Banneker too,
with knowledge of astrology,
and a photographic memory—
those designed cities,
birthed from his remarkable mind—
the deeper they dig,
the more they find us,
evidence all over the planet,
but they show us the underbelly,
and warfare,
not the peace,
and safety of Senegal,
the bushmen that represent a tiny fraction,
the jungles came after the invasions,
when no one was manning the land,
the majority is grassland,
they raided the temples of Kemet—
we were literate,
read,
and spoke many languages,
the elders warned of a force,
that would invade,
and our ways would fall apart—

I said aboriginal,
they responded with cognitive dissonance,
the ancestors told me,
without your own identity,
you will become anything,
that they tell you,
you are.

Forgiveness is a hue of black

We forgive,
not each other,
but our oppressor,
looking for equality,
not revenge,
a constitution not written for us,
the first dream we had in this country was freedom—
deferred,
the relevance of Langston Hughes,
A black man,
getting pulled over with a white woman,
in his car,
knows he is Othello,
and society is Iago,
trying to push him,
to kill her with displaced rage,
for the system,

and then himself,
with guilt in an American tragedy—
I wonder,
If,
our predicament will get better,
when their concern for our forgiveness,
of their transgressions,
meets our concern,
for our own survival,
our unapologetic voices—
say forgiving them is Stockholm syndrome,
hostages,
and abuse victims,
bonded with our captors,
captivity for so long,
my comrade said—
We forgive them because it is our nature to think they think like us,
his eyes were yellow with hatred,
at the breaking point,
when they connected with mine,
sunken deep into his soul—
I hope the ones who can't forgive Michael Vick,
and his road to perdition,
can forgive those who trained,
and released them negro dogs,

to track runaway slaves,
for their murderous exhibitions,
some were eaten alive,
Bloodhounds,
fox hounds,
bulldogs,
scotch stag hounds,
and mongrels,
treated by the same veterinarians,
who treated us on plantations,
during slavery,
because we were seen as subhuman,
not fit,
for physicians,
that supported racist ideologies,
with diagnoses specifically for black,
when being black was deemed a disorder,
by calling it Negritude,
forgiveness for Marion Sims,
who conducted experimental gynecological surgery,
exclusively on black women,
were bound to surgical tables by chattel slavery,
physical force and opium,
the drug did not abate their pain,
they became addicted to it.

We forgave,
but our distrust in seeking medical attention,
and the tag of your stigma,
don't—
but forgiveness has always been a hue of black.

Booty

Militias raided,
civilization populations,
war from greed,
seized,
and took,
the booty—
valuable stolen goods,
the bodies,
the heavy lifting,
the riches,
the genius,
and swapped it—
with labels,
named us—
the lifeless,
the lazy,
the angry ones,
embittered,
with learning disabilities,

to culturally biased curricula—
we became the pirates,
we hated—
raiding the temples,
of our women,
some of us never saw consequence,
rape has no statute of limitations,
we started objectifying,
the booty—
and labeled,
the squeezers,
to hump on,
and thots,
to hunch on—
the hoes,
no love,
the bitches,
to fuck,
from porn addictions,
calling each other *pussies,*
to encourage each other to get pussy—
by jumping in it,
hittin't it,
missionary,
pin her ankles back to her ears,
to stroke,

and poke,
doggystyle,
let her get on top,
we were passing that Kama Sutra book around in high school—
trying to kill the pussy,
but an old head told me—
you can't kill the pussy because it serves as the canal for life,
and prostate cancer kills us,
we became—
the suckas,
and simps,
the playas,
and pimps,
oversexualized—
because we think it's the only pleasure,
in a stressed life,
when real sexual appetite,
is healthy,
is spiritual,
the ritual—
of exchanging energies,
affirmations,
each pump,
and thrust,
to become a sponge,

for the consciousness,
and energy,
of that other person—
they are blessing,
or cursing you,
to create more life—
the booty.

King Tut

Rusty chains,
shackled neck to neck,
ankle to wrist,
enroute to them slave quarters—
my bleeding,
cracked,
and calloused feet,
gave me a reason—
to flash,
and floss,
when you see me,
today—
with my gold,
grind it down,
to a powder,
sprinkle it,
over my nappy crown—
spread it,
like glitter,

to serve as an emollient,
on my skin,
fashioned to jewelry,
rings for my fingers,
rings piecing my earlobes,
free niggas had gold in their grills,
to distinguish from ones still in bondage,
like Juvenile in '98, ha?
It's in our DNA to adorn—
the health properties,
too few know,
the less,
my stress,
and anxiety,
when I have it,
the more,
my immunity system,
is boosted,
the overall,
wellbeing of my spirit—
when tombs,
were dug up,
by archeologists,
in Egypt,
cursed them—

when they stole,
what royalty wanted to take with them,
to the other side—
African kings,
and queens,
didn't have gold stolen from other continents,
or other people,
they owned the gold they wore—
like the new King Tut,
Derrick Grace II,
taught me—
Keep the gold,
skip them diamonds,
because gold will always supersede,
but it's a liability,
without knowing the worth—
trade in value,
and evaluation,
get your appraisal paperwork,
and an insurance policy,
on your jewelry,
to utilize it as a write off—
the videos with fake jewels,
braggin' on social media,
you paid a hundred stacks,

to get the value of 20 back,
gold is universal—
wear it like an asset.

Soul Food

Mama's mama,
never gave up the recipe—
pinch,
and pour,
till it feels good to ya spirit,
those were the ingredients—
never tasted the same,
when somebody else tried to make it,
because she was cookin'—
with a different kind of love,
from the hip,
a few teaspoons of grit,
two cups of compassion,
put sumthin' on your feet before you catch a cold—
that stew,
with vegetables,
and meatballs,
she stirred—
could resurrect the dead in the winter,

those people ate from the earth,
but we took on their diet from chains,
and abandoned a lifestyle from our preceding freedom,
more intruders arrived—
on the shores of our health,
our food became our bondage,
whipped by diabetes,
the noose of heart disease,
and the rope of hypertension,
on a plantation of high cholesterol—
the ancestors didn't pick fruit from a produce section,
they lifted it from the dirt of God's land,
no processed,
no preservatives,
an elder told me—
if you couldn't get it from a farm a hundred years ago,
then it ain't good to eat today—
but a hungry belly doesn't hear logic,
when we got fast food 24/7,
gluttons,
better not skimp a serving,
at the buffet when I point to what I want,
or we'll swap it up,
like the Pacers and Pistons up in here,
everything on my plate fried,
walked into the kitchen one time,

granddaddy was cleaning something in the sink,
smell accosted my nostrils,
between that stench,
and what I learned what it was,
still never put any chitlins in my circuit—
but them folks had real soul food,
we don't cook no mo'—
pinto beans,
black eyed peas,
sweet potatoes,
turnups,
collard greens,
mustard greens,
beets,
and okra–
me,
and homeboy,
were chewin' the fat,
knew we had it all figured out,
after a 30-day detox—
my nigga,
this vegan thing is the lick,
talkin' shit,
with greasy lips—
rallying with hypocritical words of boycotting,
this,

and that,
for our people,
and we had just waited in line,
with everyone else,
for that new chicken sandwich from Popeye's.

Words

My vocabulary—
came from Frederick Douglass,
he fooled white boys when he was little,
told them he knew more words than him,
he didn't—
but they took the bait,
and he learned more,
when they started reciting theirs,
to show they were smarter than him.

My vocabulary—
came from my father,
he read whatever Reader's Digest he could get his hands on,
I started listening to him,
when I heard his charisma from my mother's wound—
I started at aardvark,
and started working my way through Noah Webster's dictionary,

like Malcolm Little,
after I read the Autobiography of Malcolm X,
around the same time,
they said prisons use third grade reading scores,
to predict the number of prison beds,
they'll need in the future—
low literacy levels in our communities,
wondering how words like *indictment,*
and *affidavit* confuse us,
when we break the law,
that we don't know,
then we learn how to read every book in the library,
during bids on a prison cot—
I used those words when I needed 'em,
couldn't care less when my homeboys,
told me I was talkin' too smart,
because my anger was aimed,
at the boy who thought he was superior to me,
when he said on the playground that I was—
a *nigger speaking the Englishman's language,*
found him years later,
told him the Englishman stole,
the foundation of language,
from Africans,
those words—
used to write down ten on Monday,

carry 'em in my pocket until Sunday,
reading them during downtime,
they protected me against depression,
through expression,
they allowed me to label,
therefore control,
my emotions,
when I encountered,
that state of rage,
James Baldwin spoke of,
what it feels like—
to a negro in this country,
and *relatively conscious,*
but these words mean nothing—
if I can't simplify some of the difficult things,
so that many can be reached,
because I was told—
a teacher's inability,
to teach at the level of the student,
is the curse of knowledge,
but truth be told,
I'm more eager,
to learn Swahili,
with a woman I create a life with,
to speak to our children,
in our own language.

Rite of Passage

I couldn't read when I got here,
product of the illiteracy,
in our communities,
forgotten—
these walls are for commerce,
not rehabilitation,
victim,
or predator,
the yard broke a lot of hard niggas,
who tried to knuckle heads,
locked up—
cell warriors get chin checked when that cage slides open,
when you get here—
the OG's will tell you,
that pledging allegiance to the streets,
is never a win,
because the streets are undefeated—
but those same streets,
will tell you the bullshit,

that'll get you in here—
gangstas doing bids,
hustlas in their blues,
serial killers serving all day and a night,
and survivors who kill in habitats—
of kill,
or be killed,
no way not to dance with the devil,
when you got a body,
or several—
scoundrels get to dance on the blacktop,
when identified as a diaper sniper,
treacherous guards that operate,
on the same scheme theme,
they know,
because they locked up too,
everybody figures out how to serve their time—
cowboys find out soon enough,
we lookin' for ducks,
the swindler tries to con the shyster,
the scumbag looks to weasel the weak,
the mentally ill go undiagnosed,
chatted out in the ding wing,
refusing that brake fluid,
agitators love dinner and a show,
dry snitching,

and eyeballing to seek out who is pussy,
frequent fliers fishin' for fresh meat,
too much for some,
doing the Dutch,
one big melting pot—
descendants of slaves from auction blocks,
to street blocks abiding by its codes,
intellectual property attorneys,
professors,
stockbrokers,
accountants,
real estate agents,
doctors—
all took different routes to get here,
but the most dangerous man in the world is a family man—
because he'll risk,
and throw it all away to protect his family—
seen warriors in the street,
become June bugs in gen pop—
some of these inmates ain't commit nary a crime,
imagine serving that type of time,
wrongfully accused,
a curse on their houses for Kalief Browder—
the innocence act arrived too late,
so many buried alive,

arrested joy,
the freedom of laughter,
captured—
fear morphs,
into a twisted sense of humor,
witnessed shanks pushed through flesh so many times
during contraband chorography,
you wouldn't understand why,
a man's uncontrollable giggles,
dance,
to the screams of another man on ground,
swimming away from his tormentor in pool of blood—
the mechanism to avoid going psych,
the pulse of life on the outside,
stops inside these walls,
your absence is grieved like a death,
as life goes on,
time is a tape cassette—
when you left the world,
is the point at which you'll return,
a world that doesn't exist anymore after you press play—
when released,
stuck in '97,
when he comes home in 2025,
no privacy,
showering with prison wolves,

and spider monkeys,
bend over,
and spread your ass after chow,
CO's searching for cellphones,
and pills,
in prison pockets,
after visitation,
jerk off,
and shit,
in front of each other,
animalistic,
no fear allowed,
the only option when tested,
is to fight,
or PC up,
the cagey learn to target new jacks,
solitary confinement is a meditative space,
from this zoo,
where the animals run loose,
but the hole is never a place to stay too long,
respect is king,
power is synonymous,
with a God that puppeteers the fate of those deemed weak,
one man's commissary,
becomes the tithes for the strong,

when nobody put money on their books—
the ingenuity of inmates to manufacture anything,
when time slows,
and routine is used to do that time,
a fifi bag becomes your woman,
a flick becomes your side piece,
one cellie drew a 3D woman on his mattress,
poked a hole in it,
and moaned over it to a drool,
another could defecate on demand,
smeared it on his face like war paint—
booty bandits who groom you to take your manhood,
with a cunning sociopath approach,
or gorilla force,
everyone has their game,
and the Art of War is the manual—
they took the iron pile away after a riot,
we started squatting each other on shoulders,
filled up bags of water,
and tied 'em at the ends of broomsticks for curls—
doesn't matter how many people you shot,
no guns in here,
and hand to hand combat is trumped,
when you get jumped,
a fair one with a fiend—
cry in the shower alone,

you can't take the penitentiary to the streets,
and you can't bring the streets to the penitentiary—
snitches,
disloyalty,
and backdooring,
have been going on for decades,
each generation gets the next,
infatuated with this life,
but they never told us about the bond money,
the lawyer money,
and commissary money as guaranteed fees we'd need
on the path to lock up,
and the cycle repeats itself—
my earliest memory of grandaddy was looking at him
through that glass,
I ain't coming home,
over the phone with my daddy was the last,
I couldn't read when I got here—
but I learned how,
they never taught us about the slave codes,
there was a dilemma after slavery,
because we were cleaning their houses,
raising their children,
and tilling in the fields—
those codes were a set of laws to reinstate slavery,
just freed,

we became vagrants,
no employment,
or home to reside in,
if you broke the law—
as soon as you stepped off the plantation,
then came the convict lease program,
leased you back to the plantation,
once you were arrested,
and incarcerated,
I couldn't read when I got here—
the literacy law said you could vote,
but if you could read the statement attached,
you were arrested,
because reading was against the law,
chattel slavery solved their problem,
before we could define freedom,
young black man—
this is a business,
and you are the commodity,
your self-destruction is for profit—
call home to your baby mamas,
the phone companies charge exorbitant rates,
squabble with a rival gang,
the taser gun manufacturers got it covered,
health care at your disposal,
providers secure lucrative contracts,

more beds,
mass incarceration,
more prisons,
to put on the stock market,
give you a number,
warehoused in a cell,
they keep the receipt,
I couldn't read when I got here—
I served a dime,
out at 33,
this rite of passage stops with me.

Go back to Afrika

Called him white boy,
and pushed him down,
the ghetto is a playground—
from the dirt,
but his naps,
didn't nap enough,
to be nappy like them,
when the blacker boys stood—
side by side,
like black teeth,
of a black comb—
ya daddy fucked a white bitch,
and you ain't a nigga to us,
and you a nigger to them—
skin too light to be black,
skin too dark to be white,
elders called him mulatto boy,
white boys called him a hybrid—
ostracized by one side,

rejected by the other,
ridiculed by society—
my mama said ya mama think she black
and ya daddy forgot he was black—
the linchpin of his identity,
went from compromise,
to overcompensation,
to prove his blackness,
when they couldn't accept something,
that he had no control over when he was born,
while we try to boast how Afrikan we are—
and most of us haven't set foot on the continent,
to talk that black shit.

Nothing

He said *we came from nothing*—
makin' it outta that kind of lack,
is like winning the lottery—
ticket,
or NBA,
poverty—
and crime,
are synonymous—
taught to never tell on the anonymous,
they saw shoot—
when the police tried to make a report after,
dying for the hood,
where insurance companies have stake,
the carnage—
becomes the liability factor,
a rancid environment,
ripe—
to hike everything up from store costs,
and the products they sell,

to ensure suburban areas have cheaper costs of living—
shake a nigga down,
pistol whip 'em,
and turn their pockets to bunny ears—
because the need to survive,
don't allow him to see,
through his mental myopia,
that his struggle is his recidivation,
to his nothing.

Whooping

I'll whoop you like a slave,
Nigga—
couldn't see,
that the scourge of the overseer,
from when he made one slave,
whip the other,
for running away,
became our own scourge,
when we repeated the lashings,
when we repeated the threat to our children—
nigga,
I'll whoop you like a slave—
his mama said,
I was standing right there,
she made him get naked,
as the day he was welcomed to this world,
they all whooped him too—
mama,
daddy,

his brother Ronnie,
his brother Jimmy,
his sister Keyshia—
he had forgotten to put the chicken in the sink to thaw for dinner,
fast food wasn't an option for a household with disenchanted income—
he told me at 11 years old,
that that was the last whoopin he was gonna take—
he grew up,
and became a menace to anyone who looked like his people—
he whooped niggas like slaves,
beating,
and killing—
trying to return,
what his family did to him,
and what slavery did to us in divisiveness.

Black KKK

Never seen a gangbanger slide on a KKK member—
black body,
for black body,
like a Black KKK—
twenty-one funerals before twenty-one,
imagine seeing yourself getting into a casket,
with your homie,
as an alternative to cope,
with the reality of another loss,
but knowing the set,
will put you in your own casket,
if you leave the set,
because nobody is above the set—
disciples made to knell,
to a bully pulpit,
with congregational support for backing—
no Fred Hampton,
or Black Panthers to organize for our protection,

from a gang culture that only organizes black destruction—
the lifestyle,
violates the martyrdom,
of our slain leaders,
who tried to save us—
be a victim,
or join the bullies—
needed hugs,
unrequited love,
squeezed from unbridled slugs—
breaking point,
dead homies,
but when is enough,
enough—
revenge is the reaper,
the trigger the sickle,
and doing what was done to you is never solved by retaliation—
seems like a waste of energy,
trying to convince someone whose homeboy bled to death in his arms,
that revenge solves nothing,
when your enemy adds to the cycle,
to retaliate the same way,
when their shirt has the same blood stain,

from when his homeboy got hit—
that same trauma,
made another drop his flag in explanation,
but his reasoning is seen as a weak retreat,
mentality of a buster,
casualties of gang wars—
foreign to a civilian's peace of mind,
O.G.s arrested by ways of their adolescence,
ignored pleas from their mothers early,
looked for plea bargains later,
when the white man got 'em in his courtroom,
but can't atone for the grief you caused the victims by asking for forgiveness—
obstinacy charms a refusal to denounce our deathstyle,
America's first stock was slaves—
I'd imagine the KKK has bonds in the name of crip and bloods,
because we do their work for them,
Black KKK—
black body for black body,
an adolescent game,
no compassion,
or mercy shown—
trying to seize power from a powerless state of traumatic upbringings,
PTSD from killing,

and seeing killings like a soldier,
through a brain that doesn't fully develop until the age of 25—
the innocent dismissed,
as collateral damage,
prematurely deceased,
but the biggest gang is still the police—
niggas learned gang shit from our government,
yet never learned it's illegal to be in a gang—
that's how they get you on conspiracy,
gang,
and RICO charges in court—
never learned labeling your group as a *militia* protects your rights,
never learned about a party of self-defense,
free food programs,
or how to initiate the People's Free Medical Care,
the original WIC,
free clothing program,
nor a free library—
because the set has no treasury,
no life insurance policies,
mimicking the mob,
with no formality,
unorganized—
the murderous allure,

still programs recruits,
off the strength of what the babies see,
my people from the turf—
said it's like a plague in Chicago and LA,
that we can't see,
unrepentant in our tribal role in it—
like some slave trading west African kingdoms,
that slave plantations copied,
chiefs during the colonial period of free labor,
the third mass slavery—
Arab,
European,
Africans on Africans mass slavery—
black body for black body,
victimhood is never allowed,
where power is called back to knowledge of self,
black KKK.

Last words

No name—
they called me,
Nigger boy on my birth certificate—
there's a *fightin' Nigger* in muh spirit,
cause my mama was named *Nigger gal,*
when you raped her,
stood over her,
and spat on her defenseless body—
a *runaway Nigger,*
hobbling swiftly towards the forest,
tattered clothes on muh back,
gun wound through muh left leg,
spouting blood down to muh bare feet,
them peckerwoods are gaining on their horses,
I made it to the trees—
free,
soon if I can maneuver,
and weave,
through 'em,

another *Nigger* was on a horse with them—
jumped off,
and fetched me like a hound dog,
bigger,
and stronger like a Mandingo,
they traded for,
at the auction deadline,
for their super *Nigger* slave team,
looked him in the eyes,
after we tussled on the ground—
when they kill me,
you gon' know forever,
that you killed me,
remember,
as they tie me to that chair,
and throw that noose over that thick branch to hang me,
you only proved we no better than him,
when we kill each other for him,
don't muzzle muh mouth,
right before muh body danglin',
from that tree so I can spit back at them peckerwoods,
and tell 'em,
more of me will sprout from the dirt you stole,
like seeds of retribution by the millions from muh decomposed body,
but I won't be like you,

Nigger,
I was a slave killed on the run,
because I'd rather die,
than be a slave like you,
serving Massa—
last words,
to a crooked black cop,
beating,
and shaking us down,
his name is *officer Black,*
hates his own name,
himself,
and his people the same—
like that slave catcher,
who ran down *No name—*
meritorious manumission in America,
granted to the slave,
who distinguished himself from fellow slaves,
for the slave holder's weaponry against us—
black informants in the forests,
black informants in the streets,
pitted against each other,
then,
and now—
meritorious manumission act of 1710,
the legal act of freeing a slave for *good deeds,*

by the national public policy,
still breaking up our community,
stymie to unity—
every nigga yellin' *stop snitchin'*,
every nigga sayin' they'd never fold,
never told,
in the streets,
but out of around a hundred fifty insurrections,
of slave revolts—
a black person told every time,
and were rewarded for telling on other blacks,
a system designed to dictate,
last words.

Her glory never left

She was the utopian black existence for our people,
and still is—
we forgot that she was our spaceship,
melanated Gods,
and Goddesses,
discombobulated from our universal origin—
her people were the first to circumnavigate the entire globe,
the dominion of our divine superseded mortal discoveries,
they tell you she is the bottomless pit,
but she cradles civilization in her arms,
they studied her secrets,
they harbor her artifacts,
offered her the bible,
and usurped her body,
but the world is her bloodline—
she is bigger than all of Europe,
China,
and the United States of America combined—

she is so underpopulated,
that she has the capacity to accommodate all black people in the world—
she has 60% arable land,
she has 96% of raw material reserve,
she has 48% of global gold reserve,
she has 80% of global coltan mainly found in her son of the democratic republic of Congo,
she is rich in oil,
and natural gases—
her daughter Nambia has the most fist-rich coastlines in the world,
she is rich in manganese—
iron,
and wood—
she has 1.3 billion inhabitants,
she is culturally diverse—
dancing,
music,
architecture,
and sculpture—
she's having a tech boom,
she accommodates 30,000 medicinal recipes,
and herbs that the west modifies in their labs—
she has a youthful global population with an average person of 19,

which is expected to be 2.5 billion by 2050—
she represents the future of humanity,
as She is expected to be feeding 9 billion people—
with decolonized minds,
and a strong quest for unity within her—
she will be the future ruler of other civilizations,
because the world is nothing without her—
once she gets in control of her affairs and means of population,
the rest of the world will be rendered to 3rd world countries—
China knows her glory,
as does Europe,
they invade,
and invest—
but WE don't invest in the utopian black existence,
our mother,
Africa.

Niggas

I was kid—
Indiana Black Expo,
1993—
because these white folks see us as thugs,
I don't care what ya'll think,
I don't care if you a lawyer,
if you a man,
if you an African American,
if you whatever the fuck you think you are,
we thugs and niggas to these motherfuckers,
and till we own some shit,
I'mma call it like it is,
how you gon' be a man and you starvin'—
our generation's Malcolm,
named Tupac,
was standing at the podium,
at age 22,
he knew—
that we come from a culture that has been fractured,

and never got a chance to heal,
but the world doesn't owe us understanding,
Martin tried,
to get America to see—
that *no other ethnic group has been a slave on American soil,*
tried to get America to see,
that the society of America *made the negroes' color a stigma*—
niggas forgot about the African resistance to colonialism,
like Queen Njinga Mbandi,
social media became the stage niggas act on,
niggas log on every day,
trying to escape life,
while dismissing their babies,
without knowing how to monetize the asset of time they invest in trade—
fatherless families with depressed women,
taking on masculine roles,
oversexualized seeking the only pleasure in a stressed life,
that an oversexualized nigga with no focus,
used 'em,
and left 'em for—
niggas think we were all kings,
and queens in Africa,
but most of us were farmers,
and that's how we built civilizations,

urban niggas should be ashamed,
looking down on southern niggas,
because we're all lost,
being removed from the soil of our rural roots—
Gil Scott-Heron saw winter in America,
but niggas kept going outside without a coat—
Reagonomics defunded schools,
and niggas lost jobs in the crack epidemic,
insurance companies keep niggas poor,
by pricing them based on their demographic data,
nigga communities pay 2x as much as middle- and upper-class white people—
white people want to separate from their ancestral cruelty,
but want to keep the benefits of systemic racism their ancestors set up—
if these words offend white people,
niggas will know white people are uncomfortable when the laws change—
but niggas are too comfortable,
Ama Ata Aidoo was right when she addressed white people—
you are doing it for your survival,
what is necessary,
we can't blame you for that,

because *the fact that we didn't do enough for our own survival,*
and we are still not doing enough for our survival,
that is not your problem—
the worry of the white mind is assuaged by its knowing,
that niggas look for equality,
and not revenge—
niggas sleep on the fact that in this country,
to be equal,
we must be superior,
by the circumstances we surmount daily—
niggas can't expect the invader to write the truth about niggas,
because the invader's history must justify their invasion of niggas,
echoes from the ghost of Huey P. Newton—
we do not want war,
but war can only be abolished through war,
and in order to get rid of the gun,
sometimes it becomes necessary to pick up the guns—
older generations were nourished,
by parents and grandparents in the home,
community—
niggas raise themselves now,
disconnected from a traumatized,
unheard new generation of niggas,

acting out with violence,
dilemma of black men and women,
niggas forgot Dick Gregory when he said—
the purpose is to create another God,
80% born outside of marriage,
the most revolutionary thing you can do is have a child—
but raising a child,
in a one parent household,
statistically has the worst outcome for the child—
the secret history of flooding black towns to make lakes,
the more niggas find out,
the harder it is for a nigga to love,
niggas still playin' minstrel characters—
Jim coon,
the goofy,
infantile who made white folks feel good—
and Zip coon the bully,
who wields his gun at niggas,
but won't dare revolt against white oppressors—
everything a nigga does in the streets,
are transferable skills—
niggas know more than any cooperate CEO,
niggas know accounting,
niggas know marketing,
distribution,
and packaging—

niggas get called drug dealers,
but niggas aren't the big dealers dumping drugs off in the community,
niggas love the hustle like Mitch in *Pain in Full*—
the ghetto glitterati,
makin' money,
and influencing the youngsters—
get it quick,
spend it faster,
dope fiends,
and trap houses,
starving the community over a financial misunderstanding—
media frenzy for crack cocaine in the 80's,
when Nixon's *war on drugs,*
became Reagan's campaign,
harsh mandatory minimum sentences followed,
taking black men out of the household,
no media sensation for the predominately white affected meth epidemic,
but the selling,
and using has been worse—
I'mma buy a benz,
cuz that's what niggas do,
I'mma smoke weed,
cuz that's what niggas do,

I'mma pack a gat,
cuz that's what niggas do,
I'mma get drunk,
cuz that's what niggas do,
I'm not gon' change cuz muhfuckas got money—
watching reels now,
from when Tupac was reeling,
he loved niggas,
but a nigga killed him,
and sometimes I hate niggas for that type of hate,
because hate consumes niggas,
and I don't care what niggas say,
because I see,
the genius in the message,
of a nigga like Charleston White when he's in character—
sapphire's hatred,
for white women,
and warnings of the Scottsboro boys,
only drives black boys to 'em,
Jezebel said—
your lovelorn was a curse from the ancestors,
for falling in love with the other side,
thinking you were gonna avenge slavery,
through your dick,
on a white bitch—
but the only wisdom of mammy,

got my attention,
because she stayed in their living quarters,
and knew,
best,
how they really feel about a black man—
knew the cunning vitriol,
of Amy Cooper before she threatened to dial 911—
knew the trigger,
of Timothy Loehmann before he pulled it—
feels like,
for every white that loves you,
one hundred hate you for being loved by that one,
because they're trying to survive,
genetic recessive,
one black,
one white,
and you get another black—
poor whites fear genetic annihilation,
while we hate who we are,
thinking if we act white enough,
we will be accepted by white,
but will remain black in their eyes no matter how close
we get to them—
post slavery Africans consolidated,
and were together more than ever,
the cohesion was maintained as a necessity,

through segregation—
they were a collective with self-interest,
and knew who their enemy was—
niggas don't know who the enemy is anymore,
through integration—
violence between niggas,
violence between whites,
both economically based—
but niggas are seen as the hindrance to the progress of humanity,
and us hating white people is a wasted of energy,
a waste of power,
when jobs are being outsourced to China—
and India,
nigga,
you better get with the program—
Elijah Muhammad cleaned up the disenfranchised black man,
when the black man came home from prison,
while the prophecy of Willie Lynch was still chewing away at our confidence—
we have lived in a depression our entire existence in America so who better,
to be consultants to other races how to survive—
niggas teach their kids how to be ambidextrous with a basketball,

niggas,
please—
teach them how to play chess to use both sides of their brain,
niggas need to go to the United Nations,
because Richard Pryor said there's no justice,
JUST US,
in the courts,
an epiphany in Africa Pryor had,
a voice in his head asked him—
do you see any niggas,
he said no,
the voice asked,
You know why?
Because there aren't any—
niggas are really Gods,
between Tupac and Richard Pryor.